Sarah's Crochet

©

Crochet Rag Rugs Basic
Pattern Collection

Crochet Rag Rugs
Basic Pattern Collection

© Copyright 2000, 2006, 2008
Published by Sarah's Crochet
Rag Rugs Studio
http://www.ruglady.net

Sarah's Crochet Rag Rugs Studio
© 2000, 2008, 2009

This Book Includes Patterns for:

Basic Round Crochet Rag Rug

Rectangle Crochet Rag Rug

Large Heart Crochet Rag Rug

Basic Oval Crochet Rag Rug

Slice Crochet Rag Rug

Patchwork Heart Crochet Rag Rug

China Plate Crochet Rag Rug

Harvest Crochet Rag Rug

Rippled Oval Crochet Rag Rug

Butterfly Crochet Rag Rug

Visit us:
http://www.ruglady.net

Estimating Fabric

One pound of fabric equals 4 yards. Plan 12 yards for a 24"x36" rag rug.
If you are making a 7'x9' rag rug figure .50 per square foot. Calculate: width (7) times length (9) times .50 equals 31.50 pounds.
7x9 x 63x .50= 31.50 pounds of fabric.

To Begin

Cut your fabric into 1" wide strips. You can tear the fabric also but this causes more ravelings. There are various methods to deal with the raw edges of your fabric.

- You can fold your fabric strip into "thirds" turning the edges into the middle and then rolling the fabric into a tight ball.
- You can purchase bias tape makers, from any

sewing shop, to turn your edges under.

- You can turn the edges under and use paper clips! Remove the paper clips as you crochet.
- You can crochet directly from a fabric stand, using fabric rolls, and turn the edges as you crochet. This is not as exact as the previous methods but works fairly well.
- You do not have to iron the strips.

Tip: Your most important tool is a pair of quality scissors!

Keeping Your Rug Flat

Your finished rug will be smaller or larger than the pattern, depending on your fabric and the tension with which you crochet. Try to keep your tension even throughout your piece in order to keep it flat. We add an extra sc when necessary. Trust your judgment.

"Waffling" and "Curling" are common problems for beginners. This occurs for one of two reasons:

- Curling: You are holding the fabric too tight or need to increase.

- Waffling: You have too many increases and need to decrease.

Rule of thumb: looser is better. Keep your stitches loose. Watch for gaps or pulling. If you see a gap or your piece is pulling, add a stitch. If your piece is waffling, skip a stitch. Use your pattern as a guide, and remain flexible. Remember, the thickness and textures of the fabric will vary.

Joining Fabric Strips

We recommend two methods of joining your fabric strips:

1. You can sew strips together on the diagonal, as shown on right.

2. Connect as you go: This is the method I prefer. Cut a one inch slit in each end of both fabric strips. Lay the B slit on top of the A slit. Pull C up and through both slits. Snug to tighten up. You are ready to begin.

A ⬛

⬛B   C

Enjoy!

Basic Round Rag Rug

This is a nice pattern, and easy for your first project. Cut three pounds of cotton blend fabric into 1" wide strips. Cut various lengths and join your strips. The more you alternate colors the more colorful your rug.

This works up quickly because there are many rows you work "even." The increases are clearly explained and will help those of you who have problems with "waffling" or "curling." The fabric and your tension have a lot to do with the pattern. If you feel you have to stretch to make the next stitch, add a stitch. If you see your rug is waffling and getting wavy, skip a stitch. Don't be afraid to trust your judgment. Patterns are just guides.

Row 1. Ch 3, 8 sc in 3rd st from hook, join in 1st sc.

Row 2 – 3. Ch 1, 2 sc in each sc (called an Increase), join each round. (32 sc)

Row 4. Ch 1, 1 sc in each sc. Join, Chain 1.

Row 5. Increase in every other st. Join, chain 1 at the end of each row.

Row 6. Work even. (No increase or decrease) Check your work? It is flat?

Row 7. Increase in every 6th st.

Row 8. Increase in every 7th st.

Row 9. Increase in every 4th st.

Row 10. Work even.

Row 11. Increase in every 4th st.

Check your work? Does it need more stitches?

Next 5 rows – Work even.

Row 17. Increase in every 10th st.

Row 18. Increase in every 10th st.

Row 19. Work even.

Row 20. Increase in every 6th st.

Row 21. Work even. Tie off and knot. Leave a 6 inch tail. Weave this tail behind your stitches. Weave in any loose ends.

Rectangle Rug

Chain 24 (or until your chain measures 24 inches), chain 1, turn.
Single crochet across the row making 20 sc.
Chain 1, turn.
You can vary the pattern by changing colors every few rows. Also, single crochet in the front of the chain for one row and crochet in the back of the chain in the next row. This will vary your texture and make the rug look braided. Crochet until you reach your desired length.
Finish off. Weave in your loose ends for a more finished appearance.

Large Heart Rug

Ch 24 loosely
Row 1: Work 2 dc in 3rd ch from hook, dc in each of the next 5 chs, hdc in next ch, sc in next ch, slip stitch in next ch, skip 3 ch, slip stitch in next ch, sc in next ch, hdc in next ch, dc in each of the next 5 chs, work 6 dc in last ch.

Turn to work down other side of beginning ch, dc in each of the next 9 chs, 3 dc in next ch (point), dc in each of the next 9 chs, 3 dc in next ch. = 49 stitches. Join with slip stitch to top of beginning ch.

Row 2: Ch 3, dc at base of ch, 2 dc in each of the next 2 dc, dc in each of the next 3 dc, hdc in next dc, sc in next dc, slip stitch in hdc, skip 4 sts, slip stitch in hdc, sc in next dc, hdc in next dc, dc in each of the next 3 dc, two dc in each of the next 6 dc, dc in each of the next 10 dc, 5 dc in next dc (point), dc in each of the next 10 dc, 2 dc in each of the next 3 dc. = 61 stitches. Join with slip st.

Row 3: Ch 3, work (2 dc in next dc, dc in next dc) three times, hdc in next dc, sc in next dc, slip st in hdc, skip 4 sts, slip st in hdc, sc in next dc, hdc in next dc, work (dc in next dc, 2 dc in next dc) 7 times, dc in each of the next 11 dc, 3 dc in next dc (point), dc in each of the next 11 dc, work (2 dc in next dc, dc in next dc) three times, 2 dc in next dc. = 73 stitches. Join with slip st.

Row 4: Ch 3, dc in next dc, work (2 dc in next dc, dc in each of the next 2 dc) two times, hdc in next dc, sc in next dc, slip st in hdc, skip 4 sts, slip st in hdc, sc in next dc, hdc in next dc, work (dc in each of the next 2 dc, 2 dc in next dc) six times, dc in each of the next 13 dc, 5 dc in next dc (point), dc in each of the next 13 dc, work (2 dc in next dc, dc in each of the next 2 dc) three times, 2 dc in next dc = 85 stitches. Join with slip st.

Row 5: Ch 3, work (dc in each of the next 2 dc, 2 dc in next dc) two times, dc in next dc, hdc in next dc, sc in next dc, slip st in hdc, skip 4 sts, slip st in hdc, sc in next dc, hdc in next dc, dc in dc, 2 dc in next dc, dc in each of next 2 dc, work (2 dc in next dc, dc in each of next 3 dc) 4 times, 2 dc in next dc, dc in each of next 16 dc, 3 dc in next dc (point), dc in each of next 16 dc, work (2 dc in next dc, dc in each of next 3 dc) 3 times, 2 dc in last dc = 95 stitches. Join with slip st.

Edging:
Ch 3, (dc in next dc, skip 1 st, slip st in next dc) 32 times for a total of 32 scallops. Fasten off; weave in ends.

Basic Oval Rag Rug

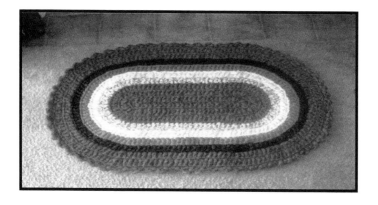

The oval rug is a terrific rug. You can make them in various color combination, change the texture by crocheting in the front and then back loops, add loops for a shaggy look, etc. Very versatile. Check your work often to make sure it is staying flat. Some ladies crochet very tightly and others crochet loosely. Some fabric is thick and other fabric is thin. This all affects the gauge of the pattern.

Estimating Center Chain for an Oval Rug

You will want to crochet oval rugs in various sizes. How do you know how long your center chain should be? Simply subtract the width from the length. Example. You want to crochet a 2'x4' rag rug. Subtract 2 from 4= 2. You need to crochet a 2 foot chain for the center of the oval and then begin increasing on the ends until your desired size.

Row 1. Ch 40, 3 sc in 2nd st from hook, 1 sc in each of the next 37 sts of ch, 3 sc in last st, working on other side of ch, 1 sc in each of the next 37 sts.

Place a marker or piece of fabric to save your place.

Row 2. 1 sc on each sc on the sides, 2 sc in each of the 3 center sc at each end.

Row 3 – 4. Work 1 sc in each sc on the sides, and 2 sc in each of the 6 sc at each end.

Row 5. Work even.

Row 6. 1 sc on sides – increase in every other sc of the 12 sts at each end.

Row 7. Work even.

Row 8. 1 sc on each side, increasing in every 3rd st of the 21 sts at each end.

Row 9. Work even.

Row 10 – 26. 1 sc in each sc on the sides, increase on each end as necessary to keep your work flat.

Slice Rag Rug

Chain 4 loosely

Row 1. 2 half double crochet in second chain from hook and in each chain across; 6 hdc.

Row 2. Chain 1, turn; 2 hdc in each hdc across. Row 3. Chain 1, turn; hdc in each hdc across row.

Row 4. Chain 1, turn; *hdc in next hdc, 2 hdc in next hdc; repeat * across.

Row 5. Chain 1, turn; 2 hdc in first hdc, hdc in next 16 hdc, 2 hdc in last hdc.

Row 6. Chain 1, turn. Hdc in each hdc across row.

Row 7. Chain 1, turn; *hdc in next hdc, 2 hdc in next hdc; repeat from * across row.

Row 8. Chain 1, turn; hdc in each hdc across row.

Row 9, Chain 1, turn; *hdc in next 2 hdc, 2 hdc in next hdc, repeat from * across row.

Row 10-12 Chain 1, turn. Hdc in each hdc across row.

Row 13. Chain 1, turn; *hdc in next hdc, 2 hdc in next hdc; repeat from * across row.

Row 14-20 Chain 1, turn; hdc in each hdc across row.

Row 21 Chain 1, turn; *hdc in next hdc, 2 hdc in next hdc; repeat from * across row.

Row 22-29 Chain 1, turn; hdc in each hdc across row.

Row 30 Chain 1, turn; *hdc in next 3 hdc, 2 hdc in next hdc; repeat across row.

Row 31-33 Chain 1, turn; Hdc across row

Finish off and weave in your ends.

Patchwork Heart

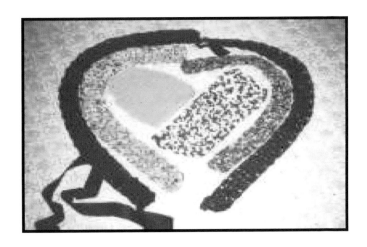

This is a fun heart and a great way to use your scrap material. It is crocheted in 6 sections and then slip stitched together. You can also use a large tapestry needle and sew the pieces together. I use a size P crochet hook for a tighter weave.

Section 1

Chain 20, chain 1, turn.
Crochet across the row using sc, chain 1, turn.
Stitch in the back loop only for a ripple affect.
Make 14 rows.
Row 15. Sc across the row decreasing by 2 stitches. (Skip 2 stitches in different places in your row.)
Row 16-18 Decrease 2 more stitches in each row.
Tie off.

Section 2

Make the same way using the diagram on page 29.
You can see this section is not as big as section 1 so decrease sooner.

Make less rows until you see your "heart" take form.
Lay section 2 next to section 1.
Can you see your heart?

Sections 3-6

This is very easy. Chain 5, chain 1, turn. Sc across the row until you reach desired length.
Look at the diagram. See how section 3 wraps around section 1? When you have the length you desire (varies according to fabric used) lay section 3 in place.
Repeat for section 4-6

This is a beautiful & striking rug! You can make it in shades of blues and greens. You may try sunflower colors. It is easy and quick and very popular.

China Plate

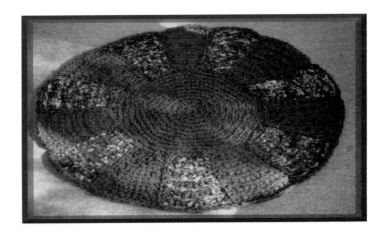

Circle

Row 1: Ch 4, join. 5 sc.
Row 2: 10 sc.
Continue for 19 rows adding sc in different places to keep your work flat.
Row 20: Dark Color.

Panels around circle

Row 1: Ch 9, 8 sc.
Row 2 & 3: 9 sc, adding sc in different places.
Row 4 & 5: 10 sc.
Row 6 & 7: 11 sc.
Row 8: 12 sc.
Row 9: 13 sc.
Row 10: 14 sc.

Crochet 12 or more of these panels and slip stitch dark color between panels. Place center in this circle and, if the size is right, slip stitch border to center in dark color. One row of dark color all around sc.

Scalloped Edge

1 slip stitch, 1sc, 1dc, 2 triple crochet.
1 dc, 1 sc. 1 slip stitch.
Repeat all around to finish edge.

Harvest Rag Rug

Petals

Make 12. Chain 8, 7sc back on
ch – no ch 1 to turn.

Row 2. 8 sc adding 1sc in the middle of the row.

Row 3. 9sc adding 1 sc in the middle of the row.

Row 4. 10 sc

Row 5. 11 sc

Row 6. 12 sc

Tie a contrasting color to a petal, and sc all 4 sides. Tie off and weave the tail of the fabric in the back of the petal. Outline all 12 petals.

Lay your petals on the floor in a circle. Have the sides of the petals touching. Now you can gauge the size you will need for the center circle. This size will vary due to different fabric thickness.

Center circle

Row 1. Ch 4, join, 6 sc into the center, turn.

Row 2. 12 sc in the previous 6 sc.

Row 3. 19 sc

Continue increasing 6 st per row, until the size fits the center of the petals.

Finishing

Use a tapestry needle with fabric ¼ inch wide or heavy sewing thread to sew into place. Outline the entire rug with the contrasting color using sc stitches. Weave or stitch all loose ends into place.

Rippled Oval Rag Rug

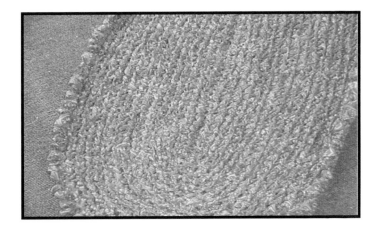

A good instructor teaches you how to adjust your patterns so you can work independently and someday create your own patterns! I didn't have the confidence to make my own patterns until I began and tried. Then I realized that all the techniques and skills I had developed over the years could be applied to rag rugs!

You can vary the texture of your rag rug simply by alternating crocheting in the front and back of the chain. Crochet one row using the FRONT of the chain and the next row crochet through the BACK of the chain.

Row 1. Ch 40, 3 sc in 2nd st from hook, 1 sc in each of the next 37 sts of ch, 3 sc in last st, working on other side of ch, 1 sc in each of the next 37 sts.
Place a marker or piece of fabric to save your place.
Row 2. 1 sc on each sc on the sides, 2 sc in each of the 3 center sc at each end.
Row 3 – 4. Work 1 sc in each sc on the sides, and 2 sc in each of the 6 sc at each end. Row 5. Work even.
Row 6. 1 sc on sides – increase in every other sc of the 12 sts at each end.
Row 7. Work even.
Row 8. 1 sc on each side, increasing in every 3rd st of the 21 sts at each end.
Row 9. Work even.

Row 10 – 26. 1 sc in each sc on the sides, increase on each end as necessary to keep your work flat.

Finishing

Loop stitch around the outside edge.

Insert hook in stitch, wrap fabric around your left index finger once more, and put the hook through BOTH loops (front to back.) Hook both fabric strips and draw through the stitch. Yarn over and pull through all 3 loops on your crochet hook. Tie off. Weave or sew in loose ends.

Butterfly Rug

See the triangles? Not as hard as it looks! Size: 28 x 42 inches

Upper Wings

Rnd 1. Ch 52
Ch 1, turn.
Rnd 2. Sc 50 sts and drop 1 sc on each end to form slant. Rnd 3. 48 sc. Rnd 4. 46 sc.
Rnd 5. 44 sc. Continue for 17 rows.
This finishes ½ wing. Crochet the other half the same way.
Crochet 2 of these wings.

Lower Wings

Rnd 1. Ch 37
Ch 1, turn. Rnd 2. 34 sc. Rnd 3. 32 sc. Rnd 4. 30 sc.
Continue for 17 rows.
This finishes 1/2 of the wing.

Crochet the other half the same way. Crochet 2 of these wings.

Body

Rnd 1. Ch 11. Ch 1, turn.
Rnd 2. 9 sc. Drop 1 stitch at every other row to form slant.
Rnd 3. 8 sc.
Rnd 4. 7 sc. and continue to 1 sc stitch.
This finishes one-half of one diamond for the body. Work the other half the same way.
Crochet 2 of these for the body. Sc in dark colors on 4 sides of upper wings, and on 3 sides of lower wings. Sl st. wings together and set in body. Sc two points in dark color that remains without a border.

Made in the USA
Charleston, SC
23 December 2010